BIG BU$INE$$

Topshop

Cath Senker

First published in 2014 by Wayland
Copyright © Wayland 2014

Wayland
338 Euston Road
London NW1 3BH

Wayland Australia
Level 17/207 Kent Street
Sydney, NSW 2000

Commissioning editor: Annabel Stones
Designer: LittleRedAnt (Anthony Hannant)
Picture researcher: Shelley Noronha

ISBN: 978 0 7502 8063 1
E-book ISBN: 978 0 7502 8542 1

Dewey categorisation: 338.7'61-dc23

Printed in China

10 9 8 7 6 5 4 3 2 1

Wayland is a division of Hachette Children's Books, an Hachette UK company.
www.hachette.co.uk

Picture acknowledgements: The author and publisher would like to thank the following
for allowing their pictures to be reproduced in this publication:
Cover: Simon Dawson/Bloomberg via Getty Images; title page: Shutterstock; p.4: Shutterstock; p.5:
Alex Segre / Alamy; p.6: Popperfoto/Getty Images; p.7: SSPL via Getty Images; p.8: Getty Images;
p.9: REX/Alex Segre; p. 10: KCS Presse/ /Splash News/Corbis; p.11: Shutterstock; p.12: Gamma-Rapho
via Getty Images; p.13: Getty Images; p.14: Shutterstock; p.15, top: REX/Richard Young; p. 15, bottom:
Getty Images; p.16: Getty Images; p.17 and p. 32: Shutterstock; p.18: Getty Images; p.19: AFP/Getty
Images; p.20: Shutterstock; p.21: Getty Images; p.22 Xinhua/Photoshot; p.23: AFP/Getty Images; p.24:
Getty Images; p.25: REX/Jonathan Hordle; p.26: Picture Alliance/Photoshot; p.27: WireImage.

Contents

Topshop today

If you go to your local city centre, the chances are you'll spot a Topshop. It's a hugely successful women's clothing chain, with more than 300 outlets in the UK and over 140 shops in countries around the world.

Topshop is found in North America, Europe, the Far East and the Middle East. Every week, around one quarter of a million shoppers visit the flagship store at Oxford Circus, London. The company has nine fashion brands, eight online stores and many concessions (outlets within department stores) and international franchise outlets (shops where other companies sell Topshop products).

Worldwide, the company employs 45,000 people in a range of jobs from design, to manufacture, distribution, transport, marketing and sales. In December 2012, Topshop and its male clothing-brand partner Topman were valued at an impressive £2 billion.

Topshop in Berlin, Germany, first opened its doors in 2013.

Women's clothes in Topshop's ever-popular store on Oxford Street in London.

One of the best-known high-street fashion chains, Topshop and Topman produce a wide range of garments, along with accessories and beauty products. Freshness and up-to-the-minute fashion are the main appeal – the collections change from week to week. For Sir Philip Green, Topshop's Chief Executive Officer (CEO), attention to detail is key. Each clothing rack is monitored weekly by size and colour to see what is selling best. With factories in 30 countries, the company can react quickly to the data and increase production of the most popular lines.

This book tells the story of Topshop from its origins 100 years ago, the launch of the brand in the 1960s and its development into a top-selling high-street fashion retailer. It looks at the ups and downs of the company, some of the key people behind the brand, and how Topshop has adapted to shopping in the Internet age.

Burton: from humble beginnings

Topshop has its origins in a company called Burton, which was founded by an ambitious teenager! In 1900, Montague Burton, a 15-year-old Lithuanian-Jewish boy, migrated from Russia to Chesterfield, northern England. A few years later, he set up Burton, a menswear business.

In 1906 Burton began to establish a chain of stores, selling both ready-to-wear and bespoke suits, tailored for the individual. In 1910 Burton moved his business to Leeds.

World War I (1914–18) proved profitable for the Burton company, which supplied clothing for nearly a quarter of the British armed forces. During the early 1920s Montague Burton started to develop his Leeds factory; within 15 years it was the largest clothing factory in Europe.

The company even did well during the economic depression of the 1930s.

By the end of World War II (1939–45), it was estimated that 20 per cent of British men were wearing Burton clothes. In 1946 Burton moved into womenswear, buying the Peter Robinson women's fashion chain. By the time of Montague Burton's death in 1952, Burton had 616 shops and was the biggest tailoring company in the world.

Former soldiers on their way home in 1945, some already wearing their demob suits.

In 1945 Burton created a demob suit with shirt and tie for returning soldiers. Known as the 'Full Monty' after Montague, the suit became famous in the fashion world and gave rise to the modern saying, meaning 'absolutely everything'.

Displaying a newly finished suit at the Burton clothing factory in Leeds.

Brains
Behind The Brand

Montague Burton
Founder of Burton

Montague Burton left Russia with £100 to set up business in the UK. He began by peddling accessories door to door and in 1904 opened his first shop. By 1929, Burton owned 333 shops and his business took an ever-growing share of the men's clothing market.

Unlike many clothes manufacturers of the time, Burton treated his workers well. He provided meals, a dentist and an eye specialist to help needleworkers suffering with eye strain. In 1931, Burton received a knighthood for his 'services to industrial relations'. He paid close attention to detail in every department, giving clear instructions for manufacturing and sales staff. Burton's careful working methods and good treatment of his workforce led to a high quality of products and services.

In his personal life, Burton loved books and he kept up ties with the Leeds Jewish community. His success afforded him a comfortable lifestyle, and during World War II, he moved to a country house in Berkshire.

During the 1960s sweeping social change took place. Young people embraced new political activities, music, art and lifestyles. Along with these changes came daring new fashions, including unisex clothes such as jeans, and brightly coloured fashion. Garments were mass-produced in factories and became cheaper to buy than ever before.

A young band wearing the brand-new jeans fashions of the 1960s.

Against this background, the Burton company founded Topshop in 1964. At first, it was called Peter Robinson's Top Shop and was located within a department store in the Sheffield branch of the Peter Robinson chain. In the mid-1970s, Topshop became a standalone (separate) shop and soon developed into one of the leading fashion retailers on the high street. Topman was launched to attract male customers in 1978. The company continued to grow in the 1980s and 1990s. Similar to many other high-street clothes retailers, it sold the latest trends at reasonable prices.

Business Matters

Mergers and demergers

The Burton Group, as it was known from 1969, expanded in the 1970s by buying other fashion retailers, such as Evans (1971) and Dorothy Perkins (1979) and merging them into its business. By buying competitors' businesses, a company increases its market share and reduces competition at the same time. Another aim of a merger is to cut costs by combining departments, such as accounting and recruitment.

In 1997, the Burton Group demerged and sold its fashion retail businesses, including Topshop and Topman, to the Arcadia Group. A demerger is when a company splits into separate businesses. It allows a big company to raise money from the sale of those businesses or to divide them up to handle different interests.

In the early 1990s, Burton hired fresh young designers to improve Topshop's range. It also invested in a huge flagship store in Oxford Street, London's prime shopping location, which opened in 1994. With five floors, it was one of the largest fashion outlets in the world.

Topshop had moved upmarket from a regular retailer to a leading fashion brand.

The front of the flagship Oxford Street Topshop.

Sir Philip Green: Topshop's top man

From 2002, Topshop was owned and controlled by billionaire Sir Philip Green, one of the richest people in Britain.

Born to a wealthy Jewish family, Sir Philip Green attended an expensive boarding school. As a child, he was extremely competitive. Green's father died when he was 12, and he left school at 15 to work in a petrol station managed by his mother. At 23, he set up a business importing and selling jeans.

Green's early businesses were a mixture of successes and failures but he travelled a lot, learning about the supply chain and other aspects of running companies.

In 2000 Green got his big break. He bought an old-fashioned department-store chain called British Home Stores, raising the £200 million cost through a leveraged buy-out. Green rebranded the shop 'BHS'. Two years later, he used the same method to purchase Arcadia, which owned fashion retailers Burton, Dorothy Perkins, Miss Selfridge, Topshop and Topman.

Sir Philip Green (standing) enjoying the good life on a yacht in St Tropez, France.

Although he is the CEO, Sir Philip Green is very hands-on. For example, just before the 2012 opening of the new Topshop store in Las Vegas, USA, he moved clothes rails around to create a higher impact. Surprisingly, he doesn't use email; he prefers to do business on the phone. In his personal life, Green enjoys a luxurious lifestyle, travelling between London and Monaco in a private jet. He throws lavish parties in exotic locations, with celebrities providing entertainment.

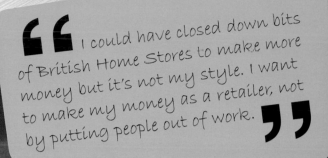

> " I could have closed down bits of British Home Stores to make more money but it's not my style. I want to make my money as a retailer, not by putting people out of work. "

Sir Philip Green

$

Leveraged buy-outs

A leveraged buy-out is the purchase of a company with a large amount of borrowed money. Sir Philip Green bought companies that were performing badly for a low cost, made them profitable and then paid off the debt. After that, he gained all the profits. In 2004, Green tried to take over Marks and Spencer, but he failed to acquire this giant of the high street.

Sir Philip Green with his wife Tina and daughter Chloe.

11

What does Topshop offer?

Topshop offers high-fashion ranges, including a wide selection of clothing, swimwear and lingerie. The brand appeals to teenagers, students and professionals through to women in their fifties – and even celebrities.

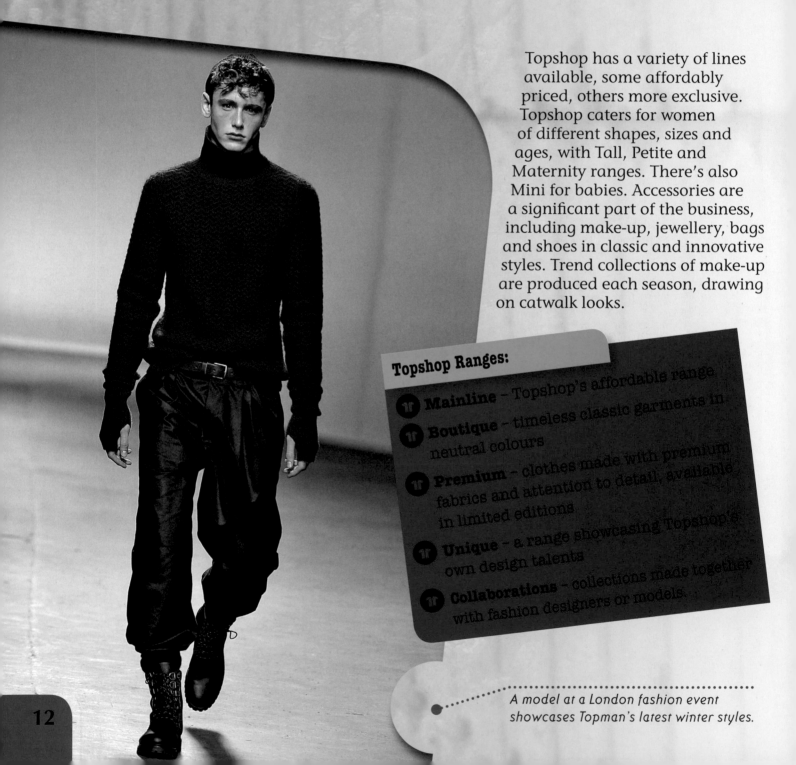

Topshop has a variety of lines available, some affordably priced, others more exclusive. Topshop caters for women of different shapes, sizes and ages, with Tall, Petite and Maternity ranges. There's also Mini for babies. Accessories are a significant part of the business, including make-up, jewellery, bags and shoes in classic and innovative styles. Trend collections of make-up are produced each season, drawing on catwalk looks.

Topshop Ranges:

- **Mainline** – Topshop's affordable range
- **Boutique** – timeless classic garments in neutral colours
- **Premium** – clothes made with premium fabrics and attention to detail, available in limited editions
- **Unique** – a range showcasing Topshop's own design talents
- **Collaborations** – collections made together with fashion designers or models

A model at a London fashion event showcases Topman's latest winter styles.

Brains

Behind The Brand

Soulmaz Vosough
Head of Topshop Personal Shopping

Soulmaz Vosough (left) with fellow personal shopper Flynn Adams in Los Angeles, just before the opening of a new store in the city offering a personal shopping service.

Soulmaz Vosough runs the complimentary personal shopping service for customers. Personal shoppers work with customers to hand-pick outfits for them, whether it's for a special event or to create a whole new wardrobe. The shoppers have a wide knowledge of all Topshop styles. They can help the customer to choose what will suit her or suggest how to accessorize her look with jewellery, a bag and shoes.

Vosough explains that personal shoppers build up relationships with customers and many come back regularly. They give hot tips on new collections so that the customer doesn't miss out on them. Vosough has a few style tips of her own: simply add heels to an outfit to add sophistication, or just update the silhouettes (clothing shapes) you wear and stick with the colours you love each season.

Topman offers a full range of clothing and suits for men. The main range follows the latest trends, and changes every month. Basic items such as T-shirts and jeans are tweaked to the current fashions. A premium collection provides refined versions, at higher prices. Topman also provides a range of suits and a Fairtrade cotton line. Topman caters to the youth market, too. It is popular with fashion-conscious teenage boys, and all Topman styles are available in extra-small sizes.

13

Topshop and the fashion world

Topshop's relationship with the fashion world has propelled it to the top of the high-street retail market. It even has its own slot in the fashion calendar. In 2005, Topshop became the first high-street brand to exhibit at London Fashion Week, showing its own line, Unique.

The company first became involved with fashion designers in 2001 when it joined NEWGEN, a scheme that supports talented new designers at London Fashion Week. NEWGEN has winners every year – previous winners include top designer Alexander McQueen. Since 2003, Topshop has also sponsored Fashion East, a non-profit group that helps emerging young designers. Every year, it offers three menswear and three womenswear designers the chance to present a catwalk collection to the international press and buyers at London Fashion Week.

Model Cara Delevingne models Topshop Unique at London Fashion Week, 2013.

Kate Moss launches her Topshop range, 2010.

Topshop has worked with many well-known designers, including Christopher Kane, Jonathan Saunders and Louise Goldin. From 2007–10 the company collaborated with supermodel Kate Moss on a 'Kate Moss for Topshop' clothing line, inspired by Moss's wardrobe. This was extremely successful, and in 2013 Moss revealed she would be teaming up with Topshop again.

Brains

Behind The Brand

Kate Phelan
Topshop's Creative Director

Kate Phelan was offered a job at quality fashion magazine *Vogue* after doing a work placement and rose to become Co-Fashion Director. After 18 years at *Vogue*, she became Creative Director at Topshop. Her role was to oversee brand identity and product development.

In 2013 Phelan worked with Google to create the first catwalk show to be fully filmed and streamed online on Topshop.com and YouTube. The team fitted high-definition micro-cameras to some of the models, so viewers had a model's-eye view of the catwalk. Viewers watching the live show could capture images and share them on social networks, and follow what was going on backstage via Instagram and Twitter. Using the Google Hangout app, fashion bloggers were invited to chat with Kate Phelan and the Topshop design team, and fans could join the discussions. The venture was hugely successful – the video stream had more than 4 million views.

Kate Phelan in Sydney, Australia after the successful launch of a new Topshop store in the city.

Online and around the world

By 2000, Internet use had taken off, and Topshop was quick to seize the opportunities, rapidly expanding its e-commerce division. The Topshop website was launched in 2000, and by 2013 it attracted 1.9 million users a week.

Although shopping online has become popular, customers still love to try before they buy.

The Internet is a major way that people discover what's on trend and having a popular online presence is vital. Topshop has a blog called Inside-Out, uses Twitter and Facebook, and has mobile apps for customers to check out the latest collections, while Topshop tumblr showcases current looks.

Business Matters

Interacting with customers online

Having a popular and entertaining online presence allows companies to interact with their customers and find out what they want to buy. Few items displayed at fashion shows are ever made in large quantities to sell to the public. At London Fashion Week 2013, Topshop adopted a 'Be the Buyer' survey to help it decide what to manufacture. Using the Google Hangout app (see page 15), fans could indicate the items from Topshop's fashion show that they most wanted the company to produce. This helped Topshop to decide which garments to make for the shops.

The company has expanded in the real as well as the virtual world. For example, the first Australian branch launched in Melbourne in 2011, and in 2012, stores in the key US market opened in New York, Chicago and Las Vegas. In December 2012, Sir Philip Green sold 25 per cent of the Topshop and Topman business to pay for the establishment of further new shops.

Topshop also has franchises around the world – it allows other companies to sell Topshop products. Companies apply to Arcadia, starting with an online application form. They go through a process to check that the market in their location is right for Topshop goods. If all goes well, they sign a contract with Arcadia. Arcadia advises on store design and the marketing team undertakes research to ensure suitable products are sent to the franchise outlet. Once its doors open, the shop receives regular shipments of the latest trends.

Sir Philip Green and his daughter at the opening of the Los Angeles Topshop in 2013.

Topshop in the community

Like most big businesses, Topshop supports charities. It's good for the image of the company to be involved in the community, and many employees are keen to take part. For example, just before Christmas, Topshop staff members run a mobile soup kitchen service for Age UK, giving out soup to elderly people.

Topshop also raises money by designing special products and donating part of the proceeds to charity. For example, the company works with Fashion Targets Breast Cancer. In 2013, keyrings were produced and for each £2 sale, £1 was donated to the charity. Talented new illustrators create Christmas cards for Topshop every year, and the profits go to Age UK. By offering low-cost products, it is easy for large numbers of people to give some money to the cause.

TV presenter Gaby Roslin (centre) at a Topshop celebrity shopping event to raise money for the Terrance Higgins Trust in 2005.

18

Business Matters

$

Sponsorship — providing funds and support

Arcadia is an important sponsor of the Fashion Retail Academy, established in London in 2006 to provide education and training to young people who are keen to enter the fashion industry. Sir Philip Green and other Arcadia directors lead special classes, and the Academy arranges work placements and supplies information about job opportunities. As well as helping young people, the project makes excellent business sense. Supporting young people who would like to enter the industry enhances Arcadia's reputation and enables it to scoop up young talent. It may select students for work placements who go on to have high-flying careers with the company.

Charitable activities can be quite innovative. For Age Concern in 2009, Topshop created the 'dress me up' scheme. Designer dresses previously owned by celebrities, such as Peaches Geldof, Nicola Roberts and Dita von Teese, could be hired for one day for £40. The dresses were later auctioned, and all proceeds went to Age Concern.

Topman has picked charities focused on assisting men; it supports CALM, an organization that aims to reduce suicide among men under 35. Topman sponsors the charity's magazine and distributes it in stores to help the charity to reach the young men who might need support. Topshop also donates garments to charity and holds sales of sample garments at its head office to raise money.

British Prime Minister Tony Blair meets students at the opening of the Fashion Retail Academy in 2006.

19

Topshop and tax

Topshop has enjoyed good publicity for its charitable work, but it has had negative press too. CEO Sir Philip Green has been accused of tax avoidance. He himself works in the UK and pays income tax (tax on earnings). But his wife Tina legally owns Arcadia, although she doesn't work for the company. Tina Green lives in Monaco, where it is not necessary to pay income tax.

In 2005, Sir Philip Green awarded himself a £1.2 billion dividend (sum of money from the company's profits). He put the payment through offshore accounts – bank accounts not in the UK – and it entered his wife's account in Monaco. So he didn't pay tax on it.

Campaigners against tax avoidance argued that the £285 million that Sir Philip Green failed to pay in tax could have paid for the salaries of 20,000 nurses for a year. In 2010, they protested outside Arcadia's flagship Topshop and BHS stores in central London.

" Any time it takes his fancy, Green can pay himself huge sums of money without having to pay any tax. "

UK Uncut, which campaigns against Green for not paying income tax, 2012

Demonstrators protest outside Topshop in 2011.

Philip and Tina Green in Monaco, where Tina is a resident. Even if she earns money in the UK, she does not have to pay income tax there.

On the other hand, Arcadia does pay corporation tax (business tax) at the full rate and has contributed £290 million a year since 2006. In contrast, around one-third of large businesses in the UK use legal methods to avoid paying as much tax as they should. Green claims that his personal finances are separate from the business and that Arcadia is more responsible than many other big firms. Sir Philip Green has said, 'We run this business 100 per cent correctly. We run it better than a public company. We know people are watching.'

Business Matters

Corporation tax

Corporation tax is payable on a company's profits from trade and investment, wherever in the world the money is made. It is also payable on capital gains, the profit a business makes when it sells an asset, for example, one of its companies. The rate differs, depending on how much profit the business made in the previous year. In the UK, there's a lower rate and an upper rate. Corporation tax is charged at different percentages around the world. A few countries are tax havens (they do not charge corporation tax), such as Bermuda, the Cayman islands, the Bahamas, Bahrain and the Channel Islands (including Jersey and Guernsey).

Workers' welfare

Topshop's code of conduct states that goods must be produced 'lawfully', 'without exploiting the people who made them'. Yet the company has been criticized for working with suppliers that do not treat their workers well.

Reports have uncovered people working for Arcadia's suppliers under poor conditions. A report in 2010 for UK television's Channel 4 revealed workshops in Leicester, UK, that appeared dangerous and cramped, and where employees received just half the legal minimum wage. Some of the clothes produced were for Arcadia, although not specifically for Topshop.

Working conditions in developing countries have even proved fatal. In April 2013, workers at Rana Plaza, near Dhaka in Bangladesh, were producing garments for Topshop among other companies. The building was badly constructed and the huge vibrating machines damaged its structure. Cracks appeared in the building but workers were ordered to return to work. The following day, the factory collapsed, and 1,127 workers lost their lives.

Many people were set free from the wreckage, but many more died in the terrible Rana Plaza factory collapse.

> **Bangladesh's tragic factory collapse earlier this year was a wake-up call about the urgent need to improve safety standards for employees in developing countries.**
>
> Justine Greening, UK Secretary of State for International Development, 2013

Following this shocking disaster, companies working in Bangladesh were pushed to improve safety conditions. In September 2013, Arcadia signed the Bangladesh Fire and Safety Agreement.

Arcadia is also under pressure to improve working conditions. As of 2013, it had not yet signed an Ethical Trading Initiative. Ethical trading means that a company expects its suppliers to work towards fair working conditions for employees.

What is Corporate Social Responsibility?

Corporate Social Responsibility (CSR) is how a company accounts for the impact of its activities on the society and environment where it operates. A company may try to reduce pollution and waste, or improve the conditions of its workers. It may back educational and social programmes in the community.

CSR can be good for business. New locations will welcome the company if it offers well-paid jobs. The company will have a better brand image, leading to more sales and attracting well-qualified staff. When employees are treated well, they tend to work hard and stay in the job.

Bangladeshi women working in factories like this one hope that safety conditions will improve.

Raising standards

Arcadia is making some efforts to improve workers' conditions. Here are some of the initiatives that they have been looking into.

Arcadia opposes the practice of sand blasting, a process that gives denim a worn or faded look. One way to create the effect is for workers to fire sand at pressure onto jeans.

The sand particles break down into fine silica particles. If workers breathe them in, it can cause a fatal lung disease called silicosis.

In 2012 Topshop carried out checks at top denim suppliers' factories in Pakistan, Egypt and Turkey, and none were carrying out sand blasting.

Topshop and Topman are also working with other retailers to produce guidelines for factories employing home workers. These employees work for a company from home, for example sewing garments. They are paid a fixed amount per item. Home workers are often paid low rates – it is hard for individuals to argue with a company for more pay, and they usually need the work. The guidelines indicate that these workers should be paid a decent rate.

Sand blasting denim to give it a 'worn' look brings great health risks for the workers, but a lot of factories still use this practice.

SWOT Analysis
(Strengths, Weaknesses, Opportunities and Threats)

Name of product you are assessing ...
Topshop Fashion Juniors

The information below will help you assess the venture. By addressing all four areas, you can make your product stronger and more likely to be a success.

Questions to consider

Strengths

Does your product do something unique?
What are its USPs? (unique selling points)
Why will people buy this range rather than a different one?

Yes. There is no other Topshop range for this age group.

Topshop is the only high-street retailer to exhibit at London Fashion Week. Catwalk looks, tailored for young bodies, will be available to pre-teens and young teens.

Topshop is hugely appealing to young people and will attract fashion-conscious kids.

Weaknesses

Why wouldn't people buy this range?
Does it live up to the claims you make?
Is it as good or better than other ranges already available?

Other high-street retailers such as H&M and Zara have cheaper fashion ranges for the 9–14 age group.

The range would need to be tried out on a focus group to check that the high-fashion garments suit young bodies.

This range would need to stand out and be reasonably priced to sell well.

Opportunities

Can the range be expanded in the future, for example, to include outerwear and underwear?
Will new markets emerge for this range?
Can it be sold globally?
Can it develop new USPs?

Yes. If the range proves popular, it will be relatively easy to expand it.

Topshop and Topman are expanding overseas, and the new range could be sold into the new markets.

Yes – as above.

Topshop could employ new designers to create garments tailored to the 9–14 age group.

Threats

Are there already too many fashion retailers in the market?
Is the market for high-fashion children's clothing less developed in Topshop's growing international markets?
Is it the right time to launch the new range?
Are any of the weaknesses so bad that they might affect the success of the venture in the long term?

There may not be a big enough market for another mid-range fashion collection.

The appeal of Topshop Fashion Juniors may be more limited in the Far East and Middle East than in Western countries.

Topshop is already engaged in international expansion so it might be a bad time to launch a new fashion range.

No. Topshop has huge production and sales capacity so the risks of producing a small range to test the waters are not great.

Do you have what it takes to work at Topshop or Topman?
Try this quiz!

1) Do you enjoy shopping?

a) No! I can't think of anything more boring than traipsing around shops.

b) Yes, I like checking out the latest trends.

c) A shopping centre is my idea of heaven. I could shop 24/7.

2) What's your taste in clothes like?

a) I'm not fussed about my clothes. I'm quite happy to wear hand-me-downs or let my parents buy my outfits.

b) I keep up with the latest styles and update my wardrobe regularly.

c) I'm obsessed with fashion! I'm constantly on the watch for the next new look and can't wait to buy it.

3) Would you describe yourself as creative?

a) No, not really.

b) I appreciate good style and I enjoy arts and crafts activities.

c) Yes. I love drawing different outfits and looks. I fancy myself as a designer – I'm always changing my bedroom round.

4) Which job environment would you prefer?

a) I'd like a nice, quiet job in an office.

b) I'd prefer to be up and about and on my feet.

c) My ideal job would be working in a massive clothes store.

5) Would you like to work with people?

a) No. I'm shy and I don't like talking to people I don't know.

b) Yes, I enjoy being around other people.

c) I'm a chatty type, so I'd love a job where I'm paid to talk all day.

6) Are you good at working with others?

a) No. I'm not keen on working in groups at school. I prefer to do my own thing.

b) Yes – I'm always the one who gathers a group together to play games at break.

c) Yes – I get on with everyone and people always ask me to help to sort out problems with friends.

7) What are your energy levels like?

a) I'm a bit of a couch potato – I prefer quiet pastimes.

b) I'm pretty active. I join in with sports and different activities.

c). I'm on the go the whole time. I love to keep busy.

Results

Mostly As: It doesn't look like you're suited to the retail business. You'd need to be more energetic and prepared to work with people. If you're really keen on working for Topshop or Topman, when you're older you could try doing some work experience in a charity shop to see how you get on in a shop environment.

Mostly Bs: You clearly have some interest in fashion and working with people, so shop work might suit you. When you're older, you might like to look for a job as a sales advisor and take it from there.

Mostly Cs: You're creative, energetic and you love fashion. If you keep up those interests, you have the potential to work at the Topshop flagship store or to be a manager in the retail business.

Glossary

asset something of value that a person or company owns, and that can be used or sold

auctioned sold to the person who offers the most money for the item at an auction – a public event to sell things

bespoke made specially for an individual customer

brand a product made by a particular company; for example, Arcadia has several brands, including Topshop (women's clothing) and Topman (men's clothing)

chain a group of stores owned by the same company

classic simple and traditional in style, not affected by changes in fashion

collaboration working with another person or group to produce something together, such as a fashion collection

concession the right to sell products in an area that is part of a larger store

demerger the act of separating a company from a larger company

department store a large store that is divided into several parts, each part selling a different type of goods

depression a period when there is little economic activity and many people have no work

ethical to do with beliefs about what is right and wrong. In business, acting ethically usually means treating workers fairly and not harming the environment or wildlife.

exclusive of high quality and expensive and therefore not often bought or used by most people

fairtrade involving trade that supports producers in poor countries by paying fair prices and making sure that the workers have good working conditions and fair pay

flagship store the most important store that a company owns

franchise permission given by a company to somebody who wants to sell its goods or services in a particular area

import a product or service that is brought into one country from another

innovative new and original ways of doing things

invest to spend money on something in order to make it better or more successful

knighthood in the UK, an award that is given for services to the country

leveraged buy-out borrowing money to buy a company

merger the act of joining two or more organizations or businesses into one

mid-range stores stores that sell items in the middle of the price range – neither the cheapest goods nor top-quality designer items

minimum wage the lowest wage that an employer is allowed to pay by law

premium selling at a higher price than normal

ready-to-wear made in standard sizes, not to the measurements of a particular customer

recruitment finding new people to join a company

sponsorship providing funds and support, for example, for a charity or for education

standalone store a store that operates alone rather than as part of a department store

supply chain the series of processes involved in the production and supply of goods, from when they are first made until they are bought or used

tax avoidance ways of paying only the smallest amount of tax that you legally have to

Trade Union an organization of workers, usually in a particular industry, that exists to improve their working conditions and pay

Index

BIG BU$INE$$

Contents of titles in this series:

ASOS
978 0 7502 8068 6

ASOS – a showcase for style
As Seen on Screen
ASOS on the rise
Nick Robertson, Founder of ASOS
Working for ASOS
Everything under one roof
ASOS across the globe
ASOS Marketplace and Fashion Finder
Connecting with customers
Sustainable fashion
Working towards ethical trading
ASOS aims for the top
Design your own ASOS product
SWOT analysis
Do you have the skills the company needs?

Heinz
978 0 7502 8066 2

Heinz: king of ketchup
Heinz starts out
The 'pickle king' – Henry John Heinz
Heinz during Depression and war
New leadership, new businesses
Going global from the late 1970s
Advertising Heinz
A wave of innovations
'Green' sauces
Heinz online
Heinz in the community
Heinz: the largest takeover in history
Design your own Heinz venture
SWOT analysis
Do you have the skills the company needs?

Manchester United
978 0 7502 8067 9

All change at the top
Humble beginnings
Fighting with debt
The Busby Babes
Life after Busby
Alex Ferguson becomes manager
The Premiership Years
Who owns Manchester United?
Behind the scenes at Manchester United
Star power
A global brand
The future for Manchester United?
Design your own merchandise
SWOT analysis
Do you have what it takes to work at Manchester United?

Topshop
978 0 7502 8063 1

Topshop today
From humble beginnings
Topshop and Topman
Topshop's top man
What does Topshop offer?
Topshop and the fashion world
Online and around the world
Topshop in the community
Topshop and tax
Workers' welfare
Raising standards
A future at the top
Create your own Topshop range
SWOT analysis
Do you have what it takes to work at Topshop?

Virgin
978 0 7502 8065 5

We have lift off
Music by mail
Top of the pops
Making movies
Taking to the skies
Virgin keeps on growing
Working at Virgin
Virgin in your home
The height of ambition
Richard Branson – the adventurer!
A company with a conscience
The future for Virgin
Launch your own Virgin brand
SWOT analysis
Do you have what it takes to work at Virgin?

YouTube
978 0 7502 8064 8

It's a YouTube world
It's good to share
Along comes Google
Content is king
YouTube in trouble
The power of partners
YouTube goes global
YouTube superstars
Behind the scenes at YouTube HQ
YouTube's greatest hits
YouTube's political and social uses
The future for YouTube
Launch the next YouTube channel
SWOT analysis
Do you have what it take to work at YouTube?

More titles in the Big Business series

978 0 7502 8041 9

978 0 7502 8202 4

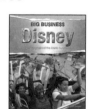

978 0 7502 8200 0

978 0 7502 8203 1

978 0 7502 8201 7

978 0 7502 7090 8

978 0 7502 7088 5

978 0 7502 7089 2

978 0 7502 7091 5

WAYLAND